Cusp

for Maggie

Graham Mort
Cusp

SEREN

Seren is the book imprint of
Poetry Wales Press Ltd.
57 Nolton Street, Bridgend, Wales, CF31 3AE
www.serenbooks.com

The right of Graham Mort to be identified as
the author of this work has been asserted in accordance
with the Copyright, Designs and Patents Act, 1988.

© Graham Mort 2011.

ISBN: 978-1-85411-548-5

A CIP record for this title is available from the British Library.

The publisher acknowledges the financial assistance of the Welsh Books Council.

Cover photograph by Helen Brock.

Printed in Bembo by Berforts.

Contents

Metalwork

Water's gleam is pewter
    the woods' alchemical copper
bronze and gold stripped
    from the trees' base-metal
that iron-old assertion
    showing through as frost scrapes
back what is rich, trivial
    and new to some lost, deeper
trope. Everything becoming
    something else: lamentation
hope, the river falling into
    its own brass throat. Sea trout
and salmon – lashing silver
    tongues that tease the weir all
night – wait unpronounced
    in the lacquered pool where
drab trees reach and meld
    across the straits below and
days of tainted foam go by
    their dappled flux always unstill.
Now it's seen me, the heron
    will unweld: all elbows and knee
joints it ratchets the uncouth
    contraption of itself into a
nickel-plated sky. Flight
    seems a doubtful art, each
wing-beat provisionally
    inventing height; everything
tentative, untested, proto-
    typical, unreal – except its bright
steel dart, acetylene eye.

Dowser

In his gawky teens he was the butt
    of wit: cack-handed, ginger, skenning
aflame with acne and a half-fledged Billy
    Fury quiff. What marked him was the lore
of hidden depths, a wire swan dipping
    on his palms, doing it for Woodbines or
Park Drive. Then full grown, runt-arsed
    a hazel fork rearing in his fists; he could
dowse anything from lost drains to
    old foundations' buried lines of stone.
Too wayward for mill work or regiment
    he never had a job, paid tax or pension;
he loved the ferret smell of cash. On
    wet days they found him in taprooms
hunched over cadged pints, talking
    elvers, ways to bait nightlines, trap moles
kill rats, lure eels with a drowned cat;
    or he'd be darting it with lads from the
cattle mart, moleskin jacket adrift, one
    eye closed to find treble six. He fished the
Greta for sea trout, poached salmon
    from the Lune, kept a sawn-off 4-10 for
snaffling grouse, started a feud over a
    man's wife at Mallerstang, divined a Roman
well at Wray and when they dug it out
    spat sour black water at his own face.
Once he found a dead girl for the police
    face-down in a foot of peat that had the
dogs thrown. It got him into bother when
    they found the gun and pheasants in his
van, when his Jack Russell bitch went
    nuts and bit a copper's hand to knuckle
bone. They let him be in the end seeing
    as he could neither read nor write nor
hardly think ahead of himself; not more
    than the next step, or the next, what with
all that was underfoot and unsaid.

Drought

It seemed a double vision: the
    natural order split along a focal
plane, those white clouds piled
    at Dunsop Bridge, May blossom
lush below, boiling from trees
    occluding them, even shrouding
that fractured half-dead thorn
    with life.

    I drove through aisles of
cream mantilla lace; a deer
    ran from its murder of young trees
a kestrel turned above a stricken
    spire of ash, hedgerows babbled
foam — burst hydrants dousing
    green fires in the bough — until
the car whined clear, revving
    climbing, stalling, froth-specked
where the moor's drift of khaki
    grass began.

    Then sunset's welding torch
at the screen showing a
    new elevation: ridges and rivers
roughcast in pollen-dusted
    bronze where insect corpses pock
the glass like stammered rain
    that fails us.

    And below, ducking under
blossom that soaps each
    slender branch's arms, Lonsdale's
wide groove pulls this tributary
    down, draws out this moment the
way all things are instantly lived
    and past and lie as unremembered

futures. Then we die, and they are
      tides of a parched mind flooding
with old prophecies: those gulls
      stacked above an empty farm, its
churns dry, its first miraculous
      enamel bath a drinking trough, its
heaps of knackered chain and
      seized pump.

      Now the home run's glimpsed
the soul's metal bead aimed
      at sunset's rust-streaked filaments.
Lakeland hills darkening the
      dazzle of scoured glass: Great Rigg
High Pike and Rydal Fell;
      the west's salt blister of sea.
Heysham's squat power plant
      its poisoned half-eternal fulmination
clear at last. Sheep glancing up
      lambs afraid and suckling, bog
cotton guttering in its own pale
      rumour of drought.

The Work of Water

We lie awake before
    the day breaks its wafer of
light, before making love;
    we listen to the rain, a panting
dove, to the work of water
    washing away gardens, its
supplications, its drowsy
    insinuations that say *watercourse*
valley, rill, stream, gulley, beck
    and *gill* (our local word
for this world-over thing) –
    all tributary to the hurried
flow of fingertips and breath.

The dove's cry comes
    again, through the flood's
garbled pronunciations
    pouring from the watershed's
ridge to the arched spine
    of the river bridge, deepening
with each moment of
    rain, each drenched syllable
deliquescing on its tongues.

Before this flood of thirst
    and touch, before there was
flesh and longing and
    blood, there was rain, there
was water perfecting
    everything that speech would
find and fill and lose again:
    river, rivulet, rill
    valley, beck and *gill.*

Triora

The house overhangs
    a valley of ruined vines
olive trees gone wild
    in their silver capes.

Soil flows to the sea
    to another century and
can't be terraced back –
    the river sucking its

mineral tang of sweat
    to another tongue. That
fleeting baffle on the
    balcony – its almost sense

of touch – is breath
    of swifts' wings, their
lungs eternal, their
    blood's fulminate of

oxygen stoking tiny
    hearts molten in the
mindless fission of
    everything: *strega*

their eyes black
    keen as if they know
all history, all futures
    in speed, in a spasm

of procreation on
    the wing, their un
anchored forms
    shearing seams of

air between the
 valley and church
where their young
 are learning this.

They scream in
 diabolic gangs, their
high cries conjuring
 newness, dazzling

as the foil of light
 glancing on amethyst
between your breasts
 that perspiration tries

to cool: I lick it from
 my fingers – salt freckles
of your hot skin – half
 expecting you to fly.

Siege

I watch ant columns enter as you sleep;
    shouts of Castilian are fading in the street
        as they advance to their redoubts; a
forward party's raiding at your knee
    their armour gleaming in faint light
        that buckles in the shutters above me.

Night-heat brings them marching to
    the bed and now a war is starting over you.
        Oh, innocent America! Conquistadors
well led! On your shoulder skirmishers
    advance to put your nipples to the
        sword or arquebus or glittering lance.

Those mortars open up a breach close
    to the dimpled back part of your knee
        whilst elsewhere, courtiers in silken
hose fawn on the gravid queen who
    cannot contradict their plot, but lays
        more grubs, endures her royal lot.

You don't wake to see them braid your
    hair in ropes that bridge the opal of each ear.
        I watch the conquest of your skin: that pair
of muleteers are bringing fresh supplies
    those sappers following a vein of blue, that
        sentry guards the closed lid of your eye.

My hand alone could clear these hoards
    scatter your spine's outriders, scouts and spies –
        consign whole armies to the skirting boards.
Instead, I watch, conspire, betray
    by stealth. There'll be rich pickings at the
        dawn: their booty, all your ransacked wealth.

Imposed, the naked wrong of war:
    new customs, inquisitions, taxes, laws
        proclaimed in vowels of a foreign tongue.
This wanton sally runs me close as I can
    get: chief suspect, self-impeached voyeur
        self-tortured whoreson of a hypocrite. I own

it all: how I let in these legions at the gate of
    night to follow them. Be still. Endure.
        Don't anger them. Don't wake. Not yet.

del Torrente Mandancio

Fish shadows over
    gravel, their blockage
        of light angelic.

Water warm against
    sun-finned skin, their
        haloes dark shivering

flames, their depthless
    souls ghosting the
        river bed.

Current, a veil
    draping my hand;
        my own emptied self

here beside me, its
    omen cast into the element
        solid as absence.

Winery Ghost

Sleep in the old winery
    has us dozing under
vaulted stone — such

strength in curvature
    time arching back to
time to begin again.

The oak bed creaks;
    past vintages fume
sour as stifled air.

You wake me to hear
    the winery ghost
our old friend, his

expirations quaintly
    hoarse, shallow breath
after breath in clinging

heat where grasshopper
    choirs pant; their winged
voices susurrate, infinitely

faint like sifting dust
    or sediment descending
clouded glass to silence.

We hadn't guessed yet
    how I was gathering lees
to cramp all inspiration

so you nudged me
    with a kind of joy to sense
the cleared wine of lost

summers, low wind in
        vines, mottled leaves
jostling clogged veins

autumn edging near to
        frost, sugar rising, each
golden orb tarnished

with rot, their noble last
        chances transpiring the way
breath fogs a mirror.

Kano

Harmattan is eyelash grit, the eyeball
skinned; grey djinns writhing through
markets, minarets and alleyways where

the poor beseech us. Nothing ceases
or can: not hunger, not thirst, the Sahel
drifting south to bury city walls, lash

sand under our tongues where words
swirl: parched leaves, fugitive birds.
Sky is a grey anvil; sun a dim sledge

of heat; trees, grey wraiths. The
Imam's voice turns us East, to the
day's long custom, history, chance.

A beggar with no hands counts naira
in the stumps of his arms, somehow
holding and counting each dirty note.

His donkey waits stubbornly, kohl
eyed, frozen-hooved through these
seconds, their whirling aeons of dust.

Okada riders gather, stare in at me
laughing through this moment gifted
from the spinning grit of the universe:

that man counting his wealth in the
hurling veils of the Harmattan, here
in Kano city where our lives came this

close then moved apart as throttles
twisted out smoke and the lights changed
so trivially he never even looked at me.

Lake Mburo

The lake is mercury smooth
    a wash of mist seeps from the softly

gullied green of hills; weaver
    birds are knotting a new day

together, one that will never be
    perfect enough for black-faced monkeys:

they call satirically, steal from
    the campsite kitchen, flaunt powder

blue balls, show their scarlet
    arseholes to the dawn. Congolese dance

music is tearing at the speaker
    cones; hippos touch their nostrils

to the liquid metal of the lake;
    fish eagles and pied kingfishers trace

themselves over still water;
    a green-backed heron is practicing

stillness – death's priestly
    similitude. Last night we sat over

unchilled beers in a hail of
    black beetles, a plague of lake flies

flocking at the single bulb.
    We watched the hills fade, heard a

storm kick-start, saw brief
    shocks of light lapping at the sky

then ate tilapia, hearing the sex
    loosed throats of bullfrogs calling from

papyrus beds where crocodiles
    lurched this afternoon and a goliath

heron stood straight as a reed
    then raised itself in flight. Now we breathe

woodsmoke, wait for scrambled
    eggs, coffee, watching a tumult of birds

a dirt-brown warthog forage
    in dirt. A barefaced go-away bird

was here yesterday, high in
    the acacia tree, silhouetted in my

shady memory of the forest
    where water buffalo wallowed to kill their

fleas, a family of mongoose
    scarpered, a black-bellied bustard ran;

at night a bush baby stared
    at the flashlight, astonished from the dark.

Now, breakfast with the weaver
    birds, the flycatcher's looping flight, the

girl who never smiles dancing
    on a patch of mud that rain has smoothed

her arms raised in a lake
    swimmer's trance to surface through

this dream at last, swinging
    hands and hips to a skipping beat;

only her feet don't move
    their bare-toed print pressed deep.

I catch the kingfisher's split
    ray of light again and know it's joy

I'm seeing, that it's complete
    and entering her face like sleep.

Catheterised

Propped in the last bed on the ward
    you exalt a bag of clearing piss the way
you once did wine from garden canes;
    miraculous, racked off to clarify, tasting
Sunday's Cana of lost country lanes.

Things surprise you now: a ward
    half-full of boys you knew at school
half-full of blokes from Bangladesh
    then this old woman shuffling in to stare
at you, whispering, *I know that face.*

You tell us how she came one night
    when wind strummed wires and windows
taut with sleet, fussed with your tray of
    magazines, then like a mill girl back
at work felt at the cotton of your sheet.

All her absences flying to the night
    she soothed you like a child perturbed
by rain and hail, then wept for someone
    gone away from her – you try to rub
her stolen kiss away but fail.

Scared in the skewed time of the ward
    you smile, say, *Now I know that lass*
how once you'd let a sparrow trapped inside
    her classroom free and how it panicked like
a troubled mind against the glass.

Imaginary

A bird is calling, nocturnal
  hoarse and unidentifiable;
a mythic owl, its face of
  frost, its yellow eye looping
over allotments, smashed
  cold frames, the fallen
asteroids of marrows
  gleaming there. Telephone
wires droop under slurred
  rain and conversation: the
call comes again, parched
  under the drifted cumulous
of sleep, the husks of our
  bodies shelled from night's
imaginaries, its fabulous
  love-making and Oedipal
dreams. We hear it closer
  now, each note scalding its
beak with some worn out
  premonition as we thresh
and turn, unthink the day
  heads pillowed in these darkest
hours, rehearsing not-being;
  eternity; supine, snoring through
a rictus mask, alternately
  tragic or smiling at the huge
nullity that we can only
  apprehend as life or its
simulacrum or endless
  night where a bird's cry grows
nearer, more vindictive
  under a blazing stellar sky.

Turbary Road

A week after the thaw
   three feet of snow still slump
      at the gate;

tracks where a tractor
   sloughed, walkers went on, a
      pheasant stepped.

The river's silver noose
   glinting down Kingsdale; Scots
      pine ragged as

crow calls. The hush
   of water everywhere and mist's
      dove-throated grey.

Hill flanks daubed with
   remnant snow; a waller and his
      wall-eyed dog

making good what slipped
   under frost, the heft of sheep
      huddling out the

worst winter in twenty.
   This is where they sledged
      turves to feed

hovel and alehouse
   hearths, burning the caked
      moor before

coal pits deepened.
   We were here this time
      last year when

I was still sick
       still wavering from life
              and everything

held the gasp of
       spring though we hardly
              knew why.

Now it's all here to dig
       and lay down again: the river's
              blue shift

snowdrops, a red-backed
       hawk gone from my hand
              paper's drift.

Manchester

Star-blind under the heat of city lights
    your fractured planes reflect in glass where
naked mannequins spend these nights

    their sexless thighs and boyish chests unsullied.
Sodium glitters in pavements' *kristallnacht* –
    but for the grace of watered beer, music hall

mongrel blood, the mills' tireless engendering.
    They came, they come, will come: remembering
Rome, Ukraine, Lagos; mourning Wicklow

    Gujarat, Guangzhou; keening for Uist, Guyana
Sierra Leone; sorrowful for Catalunya and
    Salonica; lonely for other rivers pouring them

to further shores, for skies that spill them
    light as seed. You're every migrant's halfway
home, spun from the need of their imagining

    metropolis of that fatal, imprecise desire. They
pour to your crucible: sweatshops, mills
    and manufactories, your crusted slag of languages

clay pressed to countless million bricks, cordage
    of timber, waterways, road stone, railway steel
baptismal canals of dye and filth, electricity

    radio waves and rainfall brought from Derbyshire
hills to quench your sullen foundry of the
    self. We came as if to rest and could not leave –

the moors touchable, soft as cotton waste;
    barges climbing locks from terraced streets; the
anvil, bench, the kiln, pit and lathe, insomniac

frames chattering their broadcloth to swaddle
all of empire. Tonight, neon melts winter
   streets, hums in tower blocks, lights a stainless

artistry, the museum of docks; trees bare of
   their leaves on Deansgate where grand pianos
gleam, prows cast on sacramental rain.

   You broke us, each generation; your yeomen
cut us down, forbidding trade and bread;
   you were meagre, denied us everything except

exhausted milk of our mothers' breasts
   inhuman architecture, night shifts' unending toil
flat speech, abundant alcohol, picture houses

   the wormhole of your libraries. Now you're
impossible to own or to renounce; you
   burn as a wafer, a chancre's unholy shibboleth

on my tongue; you itch in all my veins
   arsenic of smoke's slow violence. I was born
in you one August noon and dream you

   half a lifetime later: your fable of sunsets
behind mills that wore out work;
   the moon's promissory horn, its emblem

of Earth's otherness that took me away
   from you to endlessly return. Yet, come the
end, what end there'll be to know is

here for sure, what we'll toil to learn
   again is love, its dirt of ingrained truth
that all human beauty is impure.

Nocturne

The globe light shines
a whey-faced moon
    drowned in igneous rock
this rented apartment's
    bathroom floor, its sheen
of cool-veined granite.

A stray albino planet
nameless, sunk beyond
    the mathematics of focus
or taxonomy; a full
    moon's orbital perfection;
tumour in a malignant
    ocean-depth of stone
its tides pulling strands
    of weed across your face.

These are emptied
    moments; diminished
intervals, holy days
    where we stare into
our old sickness of
    longing and nothing
moves, yet the hours
    swagger to fullness.

Now this touch of
    ice on foot soles; the
light switch and its
    closure; sensations
dimming in the lost
    lives we came here to
find; this half-urgent
    quest, these choked
elegies of elsewhere.

Voices chant in
crooked streets
comradely after beer
and the big screen
after the howl of the
lost game; they begin
a song to let it fall as
silence – only its strange
language familiar.

Merlin

A sheared titanium spline
   grey blade edge flicked to air's
      thickened throat; all flickering
   instants this airborne hallucination
hunched over winter gorse –
   winged synapse-fire in the brain's
      core, a spark-point of striate
   feathered memory stropped from
hand-tipped illustrations in
   a book. I'm stumbling, eyes stung
      hands slabbed, lips numb, feet
   frost-knuckled, trudging snow
flecked heather to the road.
   Sub-zero air slows blood's murmur
      the heart's systole turgid and
   half stilled. Swaledales are sculpted
by whetstoned easterlies
   fleece-harried, hooves braced at
      gravity, the quickening suction
   of sky. Fells evaporate northward
under fallen mercury, under
   vaporising purple-smoking ice.
      The merlin swivels on planes
   of bevelled air as if I've always
known it there, like someone
   absent from my touch; the smallest
      fiercest hawk, flown from
   its fulcrum, its rapture of silence
and desire. Prying at the wind's
   seam, heat-sensing a hunger
      grounded lark, it launches
   this vision, suddenly dimensional
skimmed from the mind's
   template to kill here in heather
      scant snow, gorse; then vanish
   back onto the unturned page.

Callum at Loweswater

The boat hides in reeds, half-afloat, half-beached;
    a red tongue in water's throat, its yellow paddles

safely stashed, still wet with weed. Three years old
    his idea is deeper than a lake's rank sediments and

new as gold. His joy out-stares distance, hills'
    sagging tents a storm has reached, the way the

valley's fold takes water to its brim and tints it
    blue. The lake is licking at the shore; the boy drags

the prow about, frowning at the scale of things
    then leans from the stern as if to scan by heart

this epic setting-out he has to learn. His eyes are
    clear meltwater grey, pure glacial flow; he

looks up at you and sings *Go! Go!* wanting to
    chance high huffing clouds where green hills

and a lake of sky are twinned. The lake is ticking
    at the shore; with involuntary grace a grebe is

nodding under violet shrouds. We watch him
    play. The thought that we have sinned through

wanting more betrays your face; we're spitting
    bitter pips of the atom's core. Callum's idea zips

and skitters in his head reaching over shingle to
    horizons that never settle in a line but pullulate

and seed the fusion/fission of internal
    rhyme, waves breaking on a hull that pull every

thing towards them – life, half-life, forever –
    through the camera's single blink of time.

A Madhouse in Liguria
1955

The asylum is white-walled, the nuns
wimpled and calm, a line of shutters open
to the day as prayer books at matins.

Mild sun presses shadows into wooded
hills, the road appears as an elbow of dust
then levels at the viaduct's puzzled steel.

The nuns shave their charges who babble
a mangled language, all spit and vowels;
they rock disconsolate or laugh weeping.

Pasquale stares with grey eyes, limpid
as a saint's or anchorite's beholding
the bright inner-logic of loneliness.

The razor trails blood, foam, specks of
bristle; Sister Agatha's feet swell in laced
shoes and she tuts, holding his muscled

body lean as a hound's. Candles glimmer
in the chapel, their columns of wavering
fire glide like owls or slowly pouring whey.

A bell tolls eight o'clock. Pasquale is
silent now, as if counting to something.
He will die today on the iron bed, face

sunk into the pillow. He came from the
war, from a hamlet with only chestnuts for
bread, for *polenta*, where two men died

as partisans, their names on the bronze
plaque at the river, their women widowed
by that current never stepped in twice.

In the street they pass with potatoes
with plums, with *vino rosso*, a hand
cart of hay or basket of flags, looking

to the shutters where captives cry
like birds, where women pass at the
windows and sun scours worn tiles.

The nun's work is to right God's work
to forgive absent-mindedness, forget
imperfection with their cool touch

perfect love, with boiled white sheets
coarse soap, thin soup, with wheaten
bread and prayer and sleep and song.

Not everyone here is always lost
though most are where future cannot
be reckoned. Days slip into nights'

perpetual past: dusky phantasms of
fathers scything hay, cows birthing;
a killed hog, the well's drop and fear

of their own ghost echoing below.
Now mothers and sisters visit half
drunk on Saint's Days when they

breathe the ward's yeast of piss and
sweat, step from the nuns' blessing
into sun's fallen arc where a car

toils over the viaduct's immaculate
arch, the river narrow here, far from
the source and hoarsely roaring.

IVF

That night, seen now
    through the flawed glass
of sleeplessness, is finger
    wetted, half-full of miraculous
sudden grace, its goblet
    of frozen air ringing at the
very pitch of memory.

How quiet you sat after
    clinic, the way I drove
empty and vengeful
    at the moon – all helter
skelter in the branches –
    the hedgerows swithering;
then how a hare ran from
    a field where cows lay
sleeping on their own
    sweet muck and suckled
teats; the way you shouted
    Hare! Hare! the way it came
bounding to us like you'd
    pronounced it from that
landslide of dark in your
    head to its dull utterance
of bone on steel on bone
    that told us it was all up and
done with hare, that moon
    had gulped its wide, wet-black
eye to a glitter-ball of seed.

The car panted, the hare
    lay wrapped in silence
swaddled in the plaid
    of branch-crossed light –
moon's chiaroscuro – its
    dying breath casting a curse
of frost across the road.

You were scared wretched
        at that death, but I'll swear
on my child's life that a
        line of hares watched us
from the brightened black
        horizon, that a buck reared
and lunged and boxed
        grinning in the moon as we
dragged our trophy, its
        cricked neck and torn ear
and broken jaw, to lie with
        the jack and wheel-brace
snow shovel, spare shoes
        my father's cuffed tweed coat.

Back home we parked
        hushed the engine's moan
fumbled open the boot and
        — Christ! — that stink of hare
rank sex and blood, death's
        ether in the gunsmoke of
our breath, your hand on
        my sleeve, your eyelids flinching
from the porch light's glare.

Asleep that night, and
        deep for once, I stood on
a creaking lake-wide
        fantasy of ice, my veins
crystal, my knuckles
        numb, hearing your breath
go round me like a saw.

The paunched hare hung
        in the kitchen, its fat balls
veined and glistening; the
        moon's white petals bloomed

on window glass; a vase
      of hyacinths breathed
out their early scent.

I woke to hear the bypass
      hiss with scythes, remembered
how the final stook is called
      the hare, how all harvest is
death and sacrifice, turned
      on my back to hear a horse
cough, jackdaws shuffle
      in the flue, owls shiver
needles in the Douglas fir.

I was trying to wake, to
      shake off that dream, still
drifted in sleep, in sheets
      of creased snow, feeling air
parch my throat, blood
      tingle in my fingernails
my mind sinking on a
      tilting lid of ice – and my face
blurred you said, blurred or
      absent where I'd gone under
the hare's frozen smile.

I woke wanting you, my
      hands unraveling the silks
of your most hidden, most
      wanton self, rousing your
blush of wakefulness
      lapping your belly from the
brimful saucer of your hips
      until your body seemed
to clarify and ring, to
      burn mine, hot as ice

ringing its sunken bell
        of purest crystal, our
lips burning, ice to ice
        as we fucked away our
deaths in that obsidian
        dark and hare's beard of
blood melted to tiles
        dripped a deep red O.

Then morning's waking
        in milk-thistle light, the
curtains' gauze, the
        bed's sweet ghazal
with us in it; how you
        slept, mumbling and drowsy
and quick with child in
        our brittle room of glass.

I thought of the hook
        the gutted hare, saw
bruises risen to your
        ribs – blued iron laid
on cream skin –
        remembered that blotch
of damson, the hare's
        prodigious sex, then the
sense of something
        out there, out of reach
watching us and unafraid.

Carp at Meyrals

Grey-backed
    bronze-finned
platinum-scaled
    sculling water clouds
when sediment
    scuffs up –
gills raking out
    oxygen to their
chilled blood.

Aimless as thoughts
    for all we know;
everything beyond
    the lens of water
indifferent:
    the metal bellies
of water beetles;
    blue iris, mint
marjoram;
    the breaking/healing
edge where air is;
    a white globe curving
falling beyond
    its counterweight
as dark comes;
    swallows touching
down as death's
    beaked signifier.

What do they
    care in which
lost tongue we try
    to speak of them?
They fin an element
    beyond translation
beyond *difference*
    so unutterably.

Next

The track's desire to be elsewhere
carries her from the soaked grass
of lawns.

When she touches currant trees, the
scent will be what she remembers:
the smell of things returned to.

Exhausted from another winter
grass spikes pasture that will
waver in late-August heat.

Too bad the house is dark, ugly;
too bad workmen are replacing
stones that will fall again
from its walls.

Even daisies lie stunned by cold;
the arrogance of buds falters, the
river chokes for air — its sputter
of white water.

Whinberries rot on heather slopes;
sloes acidify, sucking her wry
mouth dry.

The past is its own season, renewable
and lost; the track soothes her — a white
scar in the valley becoming nothing else —
unable to move, taking her into
this day, the next.

Italian Hawks

They're lodged deep in the
cool of the church steeple, nested
behind an iron staple that binds
the wall into a kind of
faith with gravity.

Too fast to recognise at first —
wings and tails splayed for landing —
these kestrels are cinnamon and
grey, barred with black
and bold to feed.

Heat sends up its prayer; falcon
and tercel own the valley, following
the river's ribbon of sky where
olive trees run wild from
parched terraces.

The young wait, huge-eyed
hook-beaked, all hunger and glistening
baby-down, crowding the ledge to
snap at flies, astonished
at their own reflex.

The tercel's plumed dart
slips into sight and their high keening
starts — *Me! Me! Me!* — they pogo
at the brink in tremulous
selfishness and fear.

Something dead is tossed
to their clamour of kindling sibling
hate; they crowd the nest-hole
under the bell's cracked
angelus of jade.

Below, the organ swells with
funeral chords, the priest intoning –
his lips tarnished with death
the faithful down on their
ruined knees.

A squadron of swifts chitters
past the hawks' eyes, broadsiding
insect thermals, then lost
into a grey-green haze:
pure afterthought.

We watch the hawks feed
then leave, each chick boldening
stretching a wing, their claws
gripping an edge, then flesh
then sky, then bone.

They rend life and sense
from air; their breed is burgeoning
erasing history from stone
flying their ensign of
the present tense.

White Hill

All winter the white hill glowed
    at the window: truth towing its
        pillar of cloud; a fortress tumbled
into frozen bog. In January we
    followed a scuffed trail to the
        western flank, each footpad
petalled with blood. At evening
    snow's wavelength is amber
        sundown pinking to strawberry
meringue. Its slopes are vellum
    to scribbling hares: flat-topped
        a long bone jutting at the shoulder
where rushes spike each swallow
    hole. On the TV news we saw the
        country chilled to monochrome
from satellites in space: England's
    cur curled into its hurt. Money markets
        had failed us and politics and
war so they were the worst of
    times: death-jingo words, distrust
        the calculus of risk. Just now, when I
looked up from where a poem is
    uncoiling, line into line, not trusting
        itself to be left alone with the helix
of its language and making nothing
    happen, hedges were sketched across
        fields, cattle-breath scorched cooling
air, sheep scuffed out something
    they'd thought better of, knee
        deep in buttered snow. Now scattered
light shows all those drafts –
    so much that is impossible to
        say: *errata,* dross, each *aide memoir*
each *billet doux*, each crushed
    condolence for the coming night.

Passed

The dead are with us; amongst us
    I mean. You can tell them by the
cold tips of their ears, the yellow
    flames that issue from their lips
instead of speech, the odd way you
    still know what they mean, each one
leading us somewhere important, to
    a crime scene or some other kind
of slaughter - war or marriage.
    They walk slowly, stately, as if bearing
the weight of lilies; they pass right
    through each other and don't seem
to care, their pockets full of bright
    untarnished change or spangles
of frost. They spend their days lost
    somewhere we don't know or ever
mention; at night they throng our
    dreams under snow-tipped trees in
empty city squares that seem Eastern
    European with stray trams brightly
lit like a set right out of a spy film
    where others are always watching
from high buildings in unfurnished
    rooms. They're not unfriendly, the
dead, in their involuntary way; they
    don't mind much if we borrow their
stories or memories or ignore them
    or even reach to touch. I find your
hand to translate from sleep instead
    count your fingers like a newborn
watch the curtains breathe, rehearse
    an introductory phrase I'm everlastingly
too shy to speak, seeing them turn
    from me then disappear through their
smiles like sunset through last drinks
    or rainbows oiling the river's quay.

Black Crow

Black Crow you're door-nailed now a stiff
    kaput rogered dead to rights and how!
Arse-to-tit on the black stuff A truck or SUV
    did for you laid you low engineered your
fall though not stiff enough to stop your mates'
    croaking call *Come and play* They seem to
say it as if you could Black Crow but you're
    all spattered shite and blood got stuffed
in half a mo *Come and pay* is what they mean
    They're dining out on you even though you're
too obscene to soar or preen prefer playing
    dead incognito doggo *schtum* Black Crow
enough! You're just another bum The show
    has stopped cancelled aborted like your
plumage-sheen in speeding doors sexy self
    admiring gleam the macho stance you blagged
the carrion you snorted took you under numb
    black rubber Nicely shagged *Bon chance!*
Black Crow don't blubber you're a goner
    you're lunch your life is lopped off root and
branch and dick without prelude without
    pain so quick you couldn't muster flight or fight
Too little brain perhaps that's understandable
    an easy lapse Your breath wouldn't mist a
looking glass for all your hard-arse hard-on
    attitude Black Crow you overtook us all and
it's death it's death that won your heart that
    knocked you flat that snatched away all kerb
side latitude that made you look so utterly
    deflated superannuated a loser a gormless
twat Life's like that Black Crow You know
    it's hard to tell one chancer from the next
What made you such a class act King of the
    Undertow? More balls? Less nowse? No tact?
Tugging at hedgehog guts until a passing
    shadow pulled you in fast and slick stacked
into nil's eternal deficit where all shadows
    roost and flit Black Crow it's murder on the

hard shoulder and you've been here days ex
    airborne litter sad bum highway trash I guess
the nights are slow lonely and long without
    traffic duty or birdsong to attract/distract you
to get you through But we get along don't we?
    We get along very well Every time I cycle past
lashed in sweat I greet you with irony remorse
    regret Hail Black Crow! You beauty! You
swell! You're an institution a dark splash a
    lark a legend a landmark it's a privilege to
know No privilege can last Black Crow You're
    sadly tattered prone in the snow-white glitter
of a smashed screen battered in spilt oil fag
    ends hard porn hard-core tar one feather still
frantic in the traffic stream Black Crow I know
    you the way I knew a friend who used to be a
scream and then became a drag instead of gay
    and then was merely in my way Black Crow this
is the end of the beginning of the road for you
    What lies beyond this boundary is tough to
guess or even think or say Be brave Adventure
    on alone Don't take it hard Black Crow it's
rough luck a mantra set in stone and dropped
    into the Stygian brook Black Crow this much
is true *Carpe diem Que sera sera* I'll forget
    you I'll seize the day alright and seize the
night the new I'll thumb the future's bright lit
    passing car or magic bus and hitch right out
of here Black Crow this is your pitch your
    requiem *quietus* release your own deep shit
Death's a bitch so just decease Black Crow
    don't look at me that way Don't look at me ok?
Black Crow? Black Crow? *Touché. Touché.*

Fidelity Charm

Cradle its stasis in your hands:
    plain as a pearl, its unstrung eye
snow-blind at the mind's tundra.

Smooth and cool – an egg's
    perfection – but sterile as an ovary
masked men have sliced away.

Hold its dull orb between your knees
    burnish it, peer at drifted sand where
the hours lie, and yesterdays.

It frightens you now. So fight its slick
    of light on marbled stone, its golden
promise snug around your finger-bone.

French Dark

French dark is wilted light;
    a dark where creatures crawl
        creak, click chitinous limbs.

It's a bat-swarm, a plague of
    blood-fat mosquitoes, a fever
        swamp. French dark is a sickly

treacle of the air seducing
    cockroach hordes, a sticky
        trickle of rats in the eaves.

It's a gloomy inspissation
    at windows where jasmine
        corrupts sleep, where honey

suckle is an impenetrable
    void of memory: *nothing*
        nil, nix. French dark is the old

song of absence and benighted
    prayer. It's the hiss of blood
        in narrowed veins; the shaved

throat of harvested fields
    killed game, baled straw
        the inheld breath of woods

where a barn owl floats
    in a pale aura, its sudden
        migraine bringing you awake.

French dark has the numb
    weight of human guilt where
        the living struggle to exist like

thoughts without history;
    by day it's sun-struck glass, a
        a windscreen blazing, a straight

road, your furious blinking
    startling its after-image –
        that inky thumbprint on your eyes.

Fricative

The poem was wary but
    in love: it set out in search of its
Other, it set out on sturdy
    legs through buttercups and sheep
shit, through mare's tail and
    lady's smock and eyebright's light
hail on the grass; it scooted
    like a baby rabbit in fear of the new
life it had; it eeled through
    a hulled swan's ribs then into a blue
plastic bag, as beautiful as
    anything it had seen because everything
was good, because it was in
    love with its voice, with crushed herbs
black-bellied clouds, the
    unassailable smell of things – scents
of dirt, death or procreation –
    ewes trailing their afterbirth, dugs
tight with milk, tight as the
    poem was, sculling its skiff of images
through rivers of grass, cloud
    creeks, fjords of tidal blue sky
the hydrogen of galaxies.
    The little raft of words disintegrated
and formed again with new
    meanings or without meanings:
one minute a fridge-magnet
    babble, the next the holy bible, the
next just itself: a poem
    dissolving into sprigs of speckled
hawthorn blossom or a line
    of ducklings piping to their mother
with all the uncertainty and
    certainty of a language without
words under the lexicon
    of the clouds' dark bellies which

should by now have awoken
    the old fallacy. How cool, how
confident it was until it
    trod on something hidden, a thing
formed of metal's stiff
    grammar, its unforgiving syntax
 unfurling below a dune of
    unexpectedly hot sand; then orange
fire and the faraway sound
    of its own legs crackling, crumpling
everything into the shock of
    its body blown to bits – astonishing
stumps where its lines, caesuras
    and sunlit stanzas might have tip
toed into further doubts
    towards conclusions it could never
reach through an everlasting
    fastidiousness, the scrupulous grace
that is a kind of joy; its aesthetics
    a tremulous fluttering now, all ribbons
tattered, the way metre falters
    and is recast as fricatives pent in
the poem's mouth to
    pronounce the other selves it
sought and recognises
    here without affect; as if it had
walked calmly through
    a city's stammering walls of plate
glass, or time's reprise or
    a night-tarnished lake; as if it
had trudged into the
    vastness of nothing much at all.

Io's Sisters

The usual English summer:
    early heat stoking speedwell
      dog's mercury stealing
  a march, then months
of drizzle until rosehips
    were fading coals
      in the hedgerows
    sloes a hidden bruise
slugs cruising a lacework
    of green and bodies coming
      home under Union Jacks
    salutes, tributes, the Last Post.

Then on the fading cusp
    of August, cows calling
      nightlong into rain that
    pelted the village:
knock-kneed, teats dragging
    in mud, their lungs' bellows
      working the drenched ember
    of summer, as if Hera's spite
stranded them beyond
    phonetical love; their eyes
      goaded by flies, their tongues
    turning a hoarse cud of longing.

Even in darkness
    we question their sad
      calling with the glib surety
    of words, shaping these
smallest sounds as if glass
    had broken in our mouths
      to join up again as meaning
    measure the loss in their
inhuman mooning yet
    still fall short of ours.

Engorged, drooling
teat-sore, they drag their
banishment through wet
fields, call for their stolen
calves in pain so large
so inexpressible so deep
it erupts from the colossal
absence they circle as if
they have known in one
form, one incarnation, one
language of consonant
delight a delicacy they
could never speak in this
brute sphere, nor ever be
transfigured to themselves.

Happened

I saw the spider at its work, couldn't
    help it – even after making love – even
after Ingleborough rising through
    aluminium vapour as if streaming
bright metallic dust. The spider, leisurely
    at the kitchen window winding its sarong
around a louse like any butcher wrapping
    meat (my mother pulling me to the street
corner shop to buy lungs for the cat, to
    gawp at death). The spider toiling even
after sun had stared in at the blinds
    after the lawn's fine grass had tilted under
dew, adept at its old trade; even after
    pavements in Rangoon washed clean
the monks shot down, bullets lashed
    into the neem tree; even after Iraq's epic
genealogy of loss, its Gilgamesh of names
    inscribed upon each day where we'd buried
conscience the way a kill is wrapped –
    hidden – the spider skating over torn silk
with its haversack of palpitating life.
    There was home-baked bread on the
table, the espresso grumbling steam
    the scent of coffee, and beans dark as
healed skin. There was honey from
    Cumbrian hives varnishing the table's
oak; there was the planet warming
    up, we guessed – you'll know now how
right we were. But what you don't
    know was that a woman was brushing
out her sable cloud of hair into that
    moment's scent of lavender cologne;
that there was a tap gushing, the
    water garrulous, then silent. Do you
know what a spider does to live?
    Then imagine it. Then see the day lapping
at the window, leaking in. That was
    then, you'll say, another time, the past

scrubbing something from your
    fingernails, but wondering idly if her
breasts were warm against my
    hand, and if it happened like I said
if it happened at all: our flat
    topped mountain's blaze of silver
mist, its bog cotton, harebells
    and pyre of cloud still there to see.

Geraniums

on the Cardiac Ward

You brought them to
    my white room –
white mist outside
    and faintest trees –
three flowers purple
    as a cardinal's hood
each petal delicately
    etched
elegantly opulent.

That Indian summer
    turned to gales
chasing paper on
    the golf course;
the flowers lived
    three days then
dropped at my
    bedside
the filaments of
    each anther blown.

I swam out from
    morphine dreams
a golden river
    god roused from
sleep to see them
    scattered there
not knowing if
    I'd ever wake
with you again.

Then winter sun
    stark-lighting
each window
    white sheets
billowing to spiral
    incense-smoke
my heart wired
    to a VDU that
threw its skipping
    rope of life over
all that room's
    stalled time
and stillness
    its dreamed-over
days a fading draft
    of all I never
wanted to forget.

Montalto

The path slinks
    above stone huts;
derelict, dung-floored
    their stacks of dried
olivewood inhaling
    horizons' turquoise
their smoke of
    burnt-down suns.

Terraces fall
    to rosemary
balm of valerian
    wild marjoram;
the valley sieving
    lavender mist onto
aprons of cedar
    and bristle pine.

I'm naked in
    the river pool
its sudden green
    gasping depth
swimming its
    shoal-glimmer
dust scrim
    indigo veil of
butterfly wings
    the quenched
blade chill of
    deep sunk rock.

Martins slowmo
    above a painted
church – arrow
    tailed, white arsed –

they ride a soaring
        instinct only to rear
their young in humble
        spittle-mud below: how
like us they are to
        slum such coruscating
visions of height
        and roofless air.

Pylons simmer
        electrifying altitude;
each mountain
        pass, each scraped
out col drifts belly
        full of thunder.

Clouds saturate
        and darken; the
river's sacral flow
        quickens, deepens
to cataract my frozen
        thighs, as if I was some
spirito del'acqua rising
        you say, laughing, bent
double under hissing
        trees, your smile satirical
and unconvinced
        as summer rain.

Easter Messaging

You text me snow on Whernside hill, a
    verge of daffodils in hail – their trembling
        carillons – then black-faced ewes
    lagged by thorns in the east wind's numb
degrees of ice. A continent apart, I mail you
    the brief dusk of Abuja, the way those hills
        like *puys* behind the town go milky grey
    before a storm, that neon sign pinking a
street of royal palms, cars' headlamps
    silaging the night; then remember
        to say that yesterday I saw a net of stars
    cast from a mango hull of moon, the port
light's wide-eyed constancy. Now a
    space in which I brew black tea. Then yours
        to tell our son is home tonight to keep you
    company, down in the kitchen cutting up
courgettes. That brings the blue vein in
    his baby neck, the way his eyes and yours
        conflate in deeper brown, sheer aureoles
of watered silk. Here, the screen flares, a
crushed mosquito specks my arm; at home, the fire's
    down, he fetches logs, the door rattles in
        its frame. I'm at the window's double pane
    where a siren scours the street below, such
a long fall of heat ebbing at the glass. I'll
    send you this as well, pushing words at
        pixel-glittering space, remembering
    the moon again, its birth-marked face
yawning on the wing as we turned to land
    remembering your hand leading me to
        bed before I left again for Africa. He's stroking
    bluesy chords; your lips are wet with *Vei Cavour.*
I don't say how I think that nothing dies, yet
    see him bent at my guitar to make its birch
        throat sing, the way he will when we go under
    grass and snow to launch the spring, the
ecstatic feet of lambs that earth electrifies.

Moon Illusion

Our biggest moon all winter
ripens over Kingsdale, one day away
from fullness, left-side licked
the way a horse laps snow.

A roan mare whinnies for her
mate; I passed a horse and rider in
the dusk, remember now she
raised her whip to greet me.

Moon floats towards a snow
dappled ridge; this moment
is cochineal, sunset blazing
at a cleft in basalt cloud.

Moss on the paddock fence is
this amazing green; my heart
pads out towards night's deepest
shades, the licked moon's

illusion, the mare's inexplicable
loss; the way all sense of scale
is changed this close to dying
where everything is huge.

Cusp

December sky turns fire to earth
    Sagittarius to Capricorn, mutable
to cardinal, the archer to the goat.

Windows' white cataracts of
    slowly pouring glass are blind
to the thinning milk of dawn.

Sleep's vapour leaves our mouths:
    in mine a jagged cusp of tooth my
tongue works, raw with speech.

Five degrees of frost sift over
    fields; rabbits frozen to the road
their guts scarved out by crows.

Sky is cooling steel, the waterfall
    a stiffened crinoline; cow parsley
a paper-cut, air the thinnest blade.

Herdwicks limp between thistles
    fresh soil mounds: moles thresh
soil's black curd below, breasting

revetments, tunnelling towards
    faint susurrations where worms
glide in mucous, eating the dark.

We leave the house to itself, chose
    a route, hike all day, silent as if our
thoughts never touch, fingers

stung by cold's asp, breath's white
    grief in our hair, following the track
to the gill's ruined mines – their

lost lode, slag-scatter, milled
    spoil, stubs of clay pipes hollow as
hawk's bones. We creak over ice

panes, duck under thorn trees
	rimed with spider silk: skeins of
all their deadly industry revealed.

We walk the valley's shadow-side
	back to a house dug so deep in
clay no weight of coal can heat

its glacial stone; flames braze
	the fire-back, suck air through
cracked sash and dropped door.

No moon blurs clouds; a single
	planet sets at the horizon, its slowly
swinging plumb line telling depths

of night so cold we hardly sleep – the
	way we were as kids in our unheated
homes, the future somewhere else

but always curving back to us.
	Each word hurts my tongue which
finds a chasm in the small space

mortality begins. Tonight, we
	enter a new house, the night sky's
shattered ice of stars, only

part awake, sapped by the febrile
	cholera of dreams, our fading heart
rate, cold's enchantment, the

clock's false account of each
	inseparable moment – cusp
of love's last, longest state.

ELECTRICITY

èle'ctric a & n Of, charged with, capable of generating, operated or produced by, electricity; suddenly exciting, as if caused by electricity. – OED

"Nothing is too wonderful to be true, if it be consistent with the laws of nature." – Michael Faraday

I am the light of the world! The one
and only *Elektro Electricus Electricity!*
    I'm the path of righteousness the way of
all things The Juice! I'm the amber glow
        of a leopard's eye brindled by its own fur
I'm a white tongue forking sky with truth's
        high fidelity I'm the heart of matter –
Sensational! I'm the tongue's tender slug
        squirming in your mouth your palette's
glottal-stops stuttering your vocal chords
        fluttering under exhaled oratory speech's
butterfly flitting from thought to thought
        in the short hay-sweet summer of human
breath I'm the mouth's and the mind's
        embouchure fluting the world's cadences
Things and the space they're in all that's
        between them and beyond I'm intelligence
and what it apprehends even its own
        subtlety speed and essence I'm the bolt
of lightning in your brain *Homunculus!*
    Your ancients put me to such simple games
(between slaughter you've made them
        children at) The way dust stuck to a resin
pebble The way a rod of fossilised pine
        tar picked up a feather or a spar of jet or
raised a girl's crackling mist of hair Even
        those battle-crazed Crusaders those Mars
struck horse-borne unearthly errant knights
        were fearful of the charge that prowled
hot armour that click of blade on bone
        shocking the groom's cybernetic arm I
was bewitching daemonic elusive a
        sleeping beast or beauty highly charged
definitely on the wild side where anything
        could happen and did without your know
how or why – the way I like things best
    I was legend folklore pure faery sheer
unadulterated undiluted unaccounted
    Myth I told you the world was more than
it seemed and more various I induced

your godly instincts through naked
uninsulated *fear* lit candles in each
way-side shrine struck psalms from the
flint walls of chapels novenas from
each church's vaulted hush Respect!
But what hype! What snake-oil conning!
Cheap tricks! Such superfluity of terror
Such abundance of superstition! Such
sophistry somersaults forward rolls
and back-flips of theological minds
Such pogroms persecutions and piss
taking Such whispered prayerful
susurrations! Holy shit! The whole
religious racket from Allah to Yaweh
to sweet creeping Jesus sparked by
the odd incineration forest fire
stricken ass or burning bush! That
was more than even I'd bargained for!
I was *Other* The unknown ineffable
uncharted realm weird dimension of
the unmapped unexplored undiscovered
land at sky's end I was the cartographer's
wet dream the dragon's tail thrashing an
ocean's curdled clouds to foam I took
a long-term view so this was all a gamble
a game the first round of a hidden hand
a spot of pitch and toss just for starters
This was catch-as-catch-can and let's
face it — you couldn't No sooner did you
have me than I'd gone Here one minute
absent the next Now you see me now
you don't I'm nothing if not philosophical
Times change even if Time doesn't Only
teasing! (But you know what I mean)
Now you think that just by looking in
my direction with a little algebra the
mathematics of that juiced-up brain I
grew for you that I could be changed by
your cat-killing curiosity be somehow
different than I am? You think that *your*

inquisition might change *me?* Now listen
up and listen good! I'm no pathetic fallacy
      no abstruse allegory no mere metaphor
illusion allusion or fable I'm no pale shade
      or parable I'm not your elusive immortal
damnable everlasting soul I'm no loitering
      wraith of *your* pale consciousness No way!
It's me that cuts the mustard round here
      and pretty damned hot so get this into your
pretty little head once and for all I'm not
      like I am merely because you see me that
way No! I simply *am* Get it? Got it? OK
      I'll concede I've never made it easy for
you but why should I? I'm downright
      touchy a twisted twat a nightmare to
know Clasp me just once the wrong
      way and you'll feel the lash of my studded
belt and not let go you'll hang on for
      grim death see me glitter in the darkness
beyond life (that gutter you're star-gazing
      from) You'll find out that I'm for real I'm
for keeps Hey presto! Abracadabra! One
      flash of light just one glance in your direction
and everything's over changed forever or
      begins again The boulder skids backward
over time's scree of broken hours avalanching
      the millennial mountain burying the back
breaking ball-grinding path trodden by those
      selfish genes DNA's little scam to get ahead
There! I told you I was a god though not the
      oracular or household sort Not the meekly
crucified or doe-eyed kind More baleful
      more Baalful more the jealous type the
wrathful deity shock-jock or vengeful Jove
      Give me a rod of blue-blazing iron over a
crook of curled horn any time! *Eléctricité*
      Electricidad Elektrizität Name me if you
can It was always worth a try But remember
      I name you and name your world – the way
you sign yourself in billboard lights across

your tiny global one-horse town But what's
in a name when your idea of time is so
            temporary so touchingly tentative? Oh I
grant you were a quick learner once you'd
            bred out the ape in you dug into rocks
mined minerals felt magnesian's tug at
            iron the lodestone swinging north in its
twine cradle Earth's drawn guts quivering
            the longboats sculling through fire and
blood This way to Old Nick the grand
            paymaster! This way to cash and carry
the wages of sin! This way to the immanent
            ineffable glorious everlasting Truth! You
country hicks you hat-tipping straw-chewing
            gobsmacked stunt-pulling hucksters were
getting slick and warm at last I was in no
            hurry I'd seen it all before Another time
another place But of all the crummy joints
            in the universe you had to pick *this* one?
Play it again but get the tempo the melody
            the key the chords the sequence of the song
straight I'm pure hubris in the hands of man
            I'm Zeus' head-banging brat the thorn
scorching fire of war the double-edged double
            honed double-crossing blade of beauty
splitting the marble-white Olympian brow
            Talking of mythology (the comic-strip way
you explain things) remember Hephaestus?
            That crippled arc-welder up to no good?
And his thieving mate Prometheus? *His*
            true theft his true gift was *me* and I was
torture to him ever after Guilty as charged
            chained with iron riveted in bronze
shocked by Zeus' thunder-bolted finger
            gutted by lightning's ravening white
eagles on the drenched rocks of…Well
            yes let's get to it *eternity* Eternity?
Tell me about it! That snatched meaning
            that smugly human word for endlessness
infinity the always-vacant room beyond

the desk clerk's grasp No sooner do you
spiral out there on your pretty diaphanous
      angel's wings of thought (that luminous
flux of light imagination's voltage
      guttering in the vacuum packed space
of heaven) than you bolt back blackbox
      it with *laws* solder it with *words* the
leaden vowels of a quotidian mind Then
      when it all gets too heavy to hold you
posit a *finite* universe? Get *real*! Give
      me a break! And remember what goes
around comes around Time perhaps (you
      think) to roll out your brightest luminaries
Galvani Volta Kelvin Faraday? Why not?
      After all they tried to guess my nature
ingratiate themselves seduce then pimp
      me to servitude! Franklin spiked my
favourite most awe-inspiring party
      trick Old Faithful my oak-splitting
temple-shearing steeple-wrecking bolt
      He strung you a line in copper and I
bought it OK no problem I can be pliable
      amenable reliable when nicely asked
when your conduct is suitably aligned is
      altogether proper and correct But if it
wasn't tricks with kites and lightning
      (self-evident truths) it was some masque
of trivial pursuits — that gavotte of frog's
      legs on ionised wire — or it was the very
stuff of nightmares Frankenstein's unrisen
      clay his makeshift corpse and twitching
limbs his pearly eyes rolled back by *my*
      miraculous spark of life speech already
rotting his purple lips with loneliness Pure
      fiction! Or so you thought Man that is
born of Woman and nothing else but the
      holy word of God Man that hath but a
short time to live and is full of misery
      and cometh up and is cut down like a
flower *etcetera etcetera* What a yawn!

Come play with me and we'll see about
that with a little cryogenics but it won't
    be *your* kiss they're woken with or any
other kiss but mine *My* blue-sparking
    lips *My* speech melting their deep-freeze
complexions their slush puppy icing of
    never-lasting death What a rush! But I
digress At least you were getting a handle
    on me getting the hang of it with your
arcane paraphernalia The generation
    game in full swing now At long last you
were harnessing nature making *me* your
    tool and I was a little shocker neither
grateful nor ungrateful merely along
    for the ride (anything for a buzz!) and
time for a little bonding ionically or
    ironically perhaps You might even say
I'd become *iconic* Quite a mouthful!
    But before you knew it I was schlepping
through saltwater slinking across iron
    zinging into cells of acid slipping through
coils of copper tags of zinc anode/cathode
    attraction/repulsion You held me for the
first time speculated so that I accumulated
    and yes I stayed around for the party –
after all you had *potential* now Conventional
    current didn't get my drift but your apparatus
worked and that was all that mattered My
    induction your deduction terminals bristling
sparking at last with light with tungsten's
    brilliant heat neon's coy blush something
altogether more noble more municipal
    than curiosity or courtier's games I was
charismatic a *must* at every party! I'd
    arrived and how! You couldn't wait to
turn me on in village streets towns cities
    factories farms Even tin roofed shacks in
the middle of nowhere stuck like tiny glow
    worms to my web of light the bright net
that's always down there trawling the

blackest tides of night Darkness – that
other princely kiss – was licked at last!
     I was the original alchemist and alchemy
it was me turned base metal into cheap-skate
     gold mined earth's salts heaved scrap iron
quicker than a man or slave or horse I was
     at your service all present and correct
That's me at your wrist for instance marking
     time All that was merely the beginning
just for openers a pretty good *hors d'oeuvres*
     though the main course was still out
there somewhere beyond my electroplate
     glitter Earth's vamped-up carousel of
fairground lights What a laugh when
     Einstein went in for Bodyline chalked up
those long odds slung down that hardball
     curve at the speed of light! I didn't get it but
didn't let it get to me I hadn't peaked yet
     took guard hooked his fast stuff to the out
field the boundary fence of chaos the long
     grass of uncertainty Uncertainty? Oh yes
that became your guiding principle irresistible
     logic magnetic north of the human mind your
natural state your state of grace if only you
     knew it my *enfants sauvages* And chaos?
Those butterfly wings softly beating That echo
     of the Big Bang that whisper of the very first
word the whimper you're told was there in
     the Beginning? Well think of Shit Creek in
a barbed wire canoe Imagine hell in a hand
     cart A snowball in a solar storm! But don't
think you can talk about everything garrulous
     ape You got lucky with me that's all But then
I'm a safe bet the dead cert you could put your
     hair shirt on to trump all that bluff prevarication
doubt double-talk and second-guessing I'm
     Lady Luck herself your Ace your straight run
your prile your royal flush of electrons
     the Joker in your power pack! Why don't
you cut your losses throw in the towel

stack the deck admit that you're alone?
A loser faking it when I'm everywhere
        and everything when *I'm* the real deal?
Here's Newton in a spin struck dumb as
        a pig with an apple in its mouth Here's the
quantum level nothing quite predictable
        or safe your new-found friends those
charming quarks in jester's motley cavorting
        just where you thought you'd found the
indissoluble indivisible grain of matter
        Nothing simply *true* after all nothing
where it should be when it ought to be
        everything spinning out of logic your
physics gone autistic each particle jumping
        and skipping at the same time in two
places at once whirling inside its own furiously
        blurred helix just like the Pleiades those
seven doves Orion chased The more you look
        the more they disappear So now you've got
the universe's petticoat its red shift squinting
        in the corner of your eye? How to *explain*
all this? How to untangle all these strings?
        Holy cow! Jumping Jehovah! Jesus H Christ!
How? OK first take one extra cooperative
        cat curled in a biscuit box and drop some
radioactive isotope in there just for kicks
        rig it to a trip-hammer a phial of acid –
poor pussy! – close the lid on the whole
        caboodle count to a given number Let's
say none a nanosecond almost nothing
        nada nichts niente nowt According to
our bright sparks in the Science Department –
        and you have to hand it to them they like
a laugh – our purring friend ends up dead
        and alive at the same time *reductio*
ad absurdum! You have to chuckle It's
        enough to make a cat grin all that stuff
about multiple worlds antimatter super
        positions or to put it more *succinctly* – a
hatfull of arseholes – neither one thing

nor another Another fuckup another
facelift another frenetic false start? Or
    am I merely all things to all men? Hard
to tell eh? It's a crisis of faith a theological
    black hole the mind's white dwarf a hitch
a liturgical glitch enough to make you
    search again for that old dilettante God
And look! Here He is! Never far away
    late home again with His brandy and
cigar breath creeping back to Eden
    fumbling the re-entry latch tip-toeing
tipsy after a few aeons of interstellar
    parties bonhomie seduction booze tom
catting and good hot procreation in that
    parallel universe you dropped Him in
Look! He's home Just in time to fuck
    you up eternally and beyond to tuck
you up into oblivion Well not yet Not
    quite Maybe in His infinite wisdom His
inexhaustible patience He'll let the party
    go on late allow a few more charades a
few more centuries to play scrabble with
    the codes of life until the next the last
singular event Things are heating up
    nicely now! You'd like to change my
channel? Switch over? Switch off?
    True I can't choose you as you have
chosen me but remember I sent a billion
    shafts of pure forked fear before you
dared to call me friend Some friend!
    My caress can take the hair from your
lip or legs blaze an eagle on your chest
    tattoo *Love* or *Hate* across your fists
needle your mother's name burn a
    blood group stalag number squadron
ship of the line or lover on your arm
    I'm on your back a serpent with its
tail lost in the crack of your arse the
    rift that makes you so unaccommodated
such a bare fork'd *thing* I'm a revelation

second-sighted far out I'm omniscient
an oracle discovery itself I'm radar sonar
        a fisher of men You're the shoal and I'm
the Shoah the sting of death that tracks
        you in the end I'm your last fling the
final solution I could fry flense fricassée
        fuck you senseless or flay you in an instant
I could stretch you on my iron maiden
        that swastika of wire to shade my own
naked glare Ah! Why so suddenly afraid?
        You always knew I was well-connected
didn't you? Negative or positive? AC/DC?
        Fascist or freedom fighter? Oh! That
decadent androgyny of mine! That
        cabaret of easy virtue crotch-thonged
top-hatted thigh-booted glossy insouciant
        sexed-up *evil!* No! Oh no! Not so easy!
All that crap that bollocks that burden of
        original sin that baggage that plank in
your eye is *all* yours! In this special moral
        sense I might be called *neutral* – last irony
of iron's attraction I'm *Elektra* creation
        and chaos father-love and mother-hate
how in the end at curtain-fall the little
        stage you strut on swims in blood I define
the world – the way it is or seems to be the
        things it could become I'm flash photography
sharing secrets from the dark I'm the time
        lapsed revelation a water droplet pulsing
and bursting its trembling meniscus the
        hooves of a galloping horse a bullet striking
home I'm the finest scales weighing an
        infinitesimal load a spectrometer splitting
chemical flux an electron-microscope
        finding sand-grain worlds I'm that neon
sheen of glamour Monte Carlo Biarritz
        the kingfisher glitz of the Côte d'Azur I'm
make-believe a fairground a theme-park
        I'm Las Vegas that impossible waterless
city that desert flower with its million

gambling machines its sepals shivering
with expectation and light always light to
    hide the state of your account its tally of
black its total assets of actual and eternal
    everlasting night I'm a one-off an aberration
a revelation the First and Second Coming
    I'm immaculate Emmanuel a manifest
miracle But then again I'm ordinary like
    water coming to the boil the cellar light
left on showing cobwebs old paint tins a
    bicycle a dead man rode into the dark
I'm mundane profound the shock of
    the new I spark in your thoughts and
am your thoughts madness and its cure
    epilepsy's rip tide electroplexy's calming
electrodes clamped to the smoking pits
    of your temples I'm the reason a magnet
hates itself the way you do I'm lightning
    striking twice to fix things like nitrogen
early death insurance claims I'm the
    why in the what the way pylons stride
at the horizon bearing my gift for hawk's
    feet to curl around so carelessly Properly
grounded I'd grill them to soot I make
    your industrious little world go round –
the carbon brush the copper core (of
    the forbidden fruit) the magnet and
its bridal veil of wire Call it induction
    Call it seduction Call me the turning
worm at the heart of matter I'm every
    where and everything pervasive persuasive
restless as a shark always on the move
    Don't assume I'm in stasis when you
are Even sleep flickers with my mindless
    unvindictive rage It's me boots up your
dreams' terrors the capsized boat the
    lung of black water the lift-shaft's
hawsers and endless scream loose
    teeth the hot gun faces melted into
masks of hate wraiths that flit across

synapses the mind's marsh gas flaring
into sleep's uncensored thoughts I'm
        a sensualist a surrealist the eternal flame
the ghost in the machine I'm the lantern
        show the silent film the talkies gibbering
across your silver screen I'm home
        entertainment remote control surround
sound of the digital dream that fills your
        home with longing for *elsewhere* – palm
trees a turquoise sea a white horn of
        beach that girl miming a sentimental
song with her chromium face and collagen
        lips the last ecstatic minutes of the big
match that count down to injury time
        in the end all the same Finally I'll leave
you empty fitfully asleep in your dark
        house which is never quite dark or
ever silent since I flare in the gas boiler
        glow in pilot lights hum in the fridge
freezer rustle in the dry tick of the cooker
        clock lighting up each scarlet LED against
the endless sable frosts of loneliness Oh
        there's more! When things get tough I
get going when you forget to live I'm
        the heart's reminder the sine wave's
flickering rope of light that dares not
        dares not dares not skip a beat If you
should die carelessly without due warning
        if you overdose or sick up suicide pills
or slip the noose I'll crank you up again
        and again Stand clear! I'm what makes
you tick even when you're shunted aside
        shattered or shagged out reduced to life's
brain-dead silhouette I'll breathe for you
        The way you think of me is the way I
am Let's say I'm certain annihilation
        a bar of energy a snaking heat a molten
whiteness an eye-fusing magma a
        black numbness an eternal force spiraling
the dawn of the universe still echoing

with light I'm albino without pigment
invisible to your naked eye too good
     to be true too true to be good I'm a
secret that just couldn't be kept There
     I go again getting my hair off! I'm a
lethal dose though I'm not just or justice
     I can't think straight know zip feel
nothing understand less I'm a numpty
     a dickhead a dumbo dead as a doornail
one minute a real livewire the next! I'm
     what can't be seen high-tension the
beginning the source of attraction male
     and female the way opposites pull close
and couple I'm the kiss coitus the act
     the very spasm of love I'm the fearful
shock of hate that raises your electrostatic
     hair Without me no matter no universe
no space (so to speak) no time (worth
     mentioning) not one echo *Listen Listen*
of anything Not one single moment to
     uselessly and meaninglessly while away
In the Beginning? Light heat energy
     speed distance – *electricity!* – all in less
than the instant there was no time to
     measure or formulate the idea the word
to tell how *anything* became *something*
     What else? Protons electrons neutrons
atoms molecules *matter* – all that dust
     and gas fire and ice water and steam the
piss and wind of space-time dollops of *stuff*
     whole families flying their wall–of–death
orbits showing off in the atom's introverted
     universe and that other universe out there
its infinite scale billowing still Call me an
     old trouper trust me believe me I know
I was there when the match kicked off I
     laid on the fireworks got the show on the
road and a long way down it It was me
     held things *together* Before that? Search
me! But you of all beings should at least

hazard a guess after all guessing's what
you're good at Lucky Man Just think Yes
        think! Most of matter most of *everything*
is *nothing* space we can't cross neither
        you to me nor me to you nor you to
each other You need me and I'll admit
        for once that I need you Touching eh?
Let's hold hands tie the knot do the deed
        get hitched let's be a source of friction
of inspiration to each other I'll be your
        Muse if you'll be mine Touch me just
once plug in and I'll let rip a sheet of
        pure incandescence to seal the deal Keep
looking for me if I seem to be a little lost
        it's just that I'm pre-occupied the spin
doctor of time and space busy finessing
        the black holes between stars that universe
you think is there and just like it is and
        like no other because *you* live in its cosmic
imperative How could it be otherwise?
        Do you get it yet? Understand? Are you
savvy? Switched on? Do you read me?
        Dig me? Cotton on? Are you in the loop?
Wired-up yet to any of this? You should be
        After all I'm perception your hearing and
all that's heard the spheres and their music
        traveling towards your ear's smithy
of bone I'm vision and all that's seen —
        those pink clouds at sunset the follicles
on your arm your lover's face leaning
        close I'm the feel of things touched their
smell and taste sensations you have precious
        few words for I'm your mind all that it has
thought reflected synthesised I am therefore
        you are *Ergo* I am beauty itself and truth
Narcissus was a beginner at this a vain kid
        with his zitty mug hung over a puddle Imagine
seeing yourself in the galaxies in a cascading
        lake of stars! Imagine if I let you the echo
of eternity in your own voice I'm a frightener

a head-fucker a fulgurite – that spar of fused
earth glassy minerals melted sand lightning's
 smouldering totem potent with spent force
The ultimate hard-on! I'm a currency never
 spent Alpha and Omega the flash of light
and vaulted dark the spark of motion the
 shock of stasis I'm that halo of Christmas
lights flickering in snow-bound city squares
 I haunt that steel ship signaling far out
beyond the lighthouse blinking at the land's
 last treacherous tip its portholes drilled with
yellow light its sacrificial diodes shedding
 my charge I'm ball-lightning black lightning
sheet lightning St Elmo's fire the Zodiac's
 hidden sign Arachne spinning the silver
rigging of the universe I was the jism in
 that primordial soup I began the molecule's
fumbling dance the double-helix the single
 celled self-assembling antecedent of every
thing that crawls grows divides couples fucks
 kills and breathes across this Earth What
would you be without me? And who? Too
 late now to pull back to change that mutable
little mind I'm a current flowing too fast
 towing you beyond the dark I'm the white
hot filament you'd go blind without the glow
 in your cities that can't hold a candle yet
to all the centuries of night I'm atavistic
 futuristic the skull beneath the skin the
brain beneath the flying helmet Gagarin
 watching Earth spin under his ownsome
lonesome gaze I'm the life-force in the
 probe that travels out of sight and mind
sending its gaseous pictures home even
 when home is the ember of its own destiny
the sun's ashen hearth I'm words under
 your tongue I'm speech gabbling across
your tiny globe I'm the message and the
 medium the meaning of Marconi's code
S for SOS Without me imagine dumbness

the iced-up grip of time the world's mouth
frozen shut the roses black the TV screens'
     flickering storms of static dying blank as
unborn minds Remember this is the way
     we were the way you will be in the end
I'm the lit skyscraper at night temple of
     aspiration and hope its tessellation above
sodium canyons where traffic is flotsam
     on the street's rising flood of light I'm aerial
joystick and cruise control the voice in the
     black box the gadfly searching for the
runway's golden track of light until I call it
     down to Earth All that make me essential
indispensable dependable? Without me
     you'd fall again just as you fell without
me at the start from your idyll your Arcadian
     state of grace Is that it? You've learned to
trust me as a friend at last? After all's said
     and done I'm a distraction I'm recreation
the disco beat the dance floor's strobe-lit
     gush of sweat the guitar screaming
feedback's what really turns me on I'm
     easily ecstatic aesthetic all heart the
cardioid microphone in the singer's hands
     lighting studio dials and digital displays
Her voice is beautiful you think so store
     it in an analogue of sound code it into
memory chips replay its endless loveliness
     unlock the moment steal away time still
it or stand it on its head no distortion or
     surface noise to distance you Kill time
like this if you dare Kill it with the naked
     beauty of song I'm the impulse of desire
flaring dictating the motion of a hand to
     fair or foul I'm the motive and the deed
the universal yeast the body electric a kind
     of *poetry* I'm the fence guarding cattle
the torturer's goad the stun-gun the field
     telephone ratcheting your cruciform body's
exquisite agony to give away everything

or make it up to lie/not lie disclose reveal
make known expose dissemble No not
      that! To sweat it out and against all odds
survive I'm terror The illiterate random
      force of darkness the fused relay scrambled
wires the psychosis at the heart of things
      I'm the suicide bomber standing beside
you his quiet smile of fulfilment the
      madman's pencil torch probing your door
the voice on the 'phone the death threat
      and the silence buzzing in its wake I'm
the cursor blinking at your name the
      bureaucrat's deadly cognisance the laser
in the surgeon's hands the killer's loop of
      flex the sweat on your temple conducive
to pain I'm impartial static or stealthy
      still or on the move micro or macro
a hundred volts a thousand amps a million
      watts the shadow of a doubt the merest
flicker of interest in a bored mind I'm
      the Death Row chair – Old Yeller – with its
straps electrode gel and stubborn stains
      its voltage frying the condemned convict's
memories of life his hopes and loves his
      pinned limbs and frantic brains I'm X-rays
the CT scan the VDU the mind-forg'd
      manacles of man I'm information and
plenty of it a billion bits of data hard fact
      soft porn paedophilia fiction figures
formulae blarney and bullshit all the same
      It's for me you've chained waterfalls
harnessed tides made isotopes undress stoked
      the turbine laid that row of white crosses
turning on the hill to farm the wind's memory
      of flight I'm the Sargasso-seeking eel
coiling in darkness the weirdness of low
      level life a bottom-feeder glittering under
that tonnage of oceanic dark the monkfish
      the electric ray the angler fish dangling
his bulb in the sea's sordid tenement I'm

81

all that deep-down bio-luminescence the
blue glow of the depths I'm pressure
accumulating charge and discharge I'm
the way of things down there Up here
I'm the Gulag Auschwitz's gateway its
necklet of wire its torque of watchtowers
its twisting force — *Arbeit Macht Frei* — I'm
its glittering Himmelstrasse one step one
touch from heaven I'm that sick yellow
light in the prison cell — Lubyanka's naked
bulb — I'm at your service SS Gestapo CIA
KGB NKVD a Special Branch on a very
special tree I'm a place name lit up at the
dead of night the frost-spangled platform
where dogs snarl on the handler's chain-link
leash I'm the glimmer of tracks converging
the screech of rolling stock the slow
thunder and thud of destination destiny
that apotheosis of scribbled smoke I
won't say you got that wrong or went
too far It was your artwork after all It
haunts you now your symphony your
fugue in human staves clotted notes the
future figured the blackout where your
numbed hands thrust up stiffened from
their self-dug grave All this from simply
fiddling with the fusebox from fumbling
blindly in the dark! Who's there? A
shaman a sadhu a sheister a bombshell
a barfly a lady-killing crooner a Janus
faced cruiser a queer cunt a crazy coot
the delivery guy with a pretty smart
cookie Enola Gay Fat Man Little Boy
Hiroshima Nagasaki Oh fission fusion
fission! How to choose? You peeled me
like a yam squeezed Armageddon till the
pips squeaked vaporising everything
to blind energy pure milk of darkness —
$E=MC^2$ — Pure jazz! Everything leveled
polluted razed humanity's house poisoned

to its half-life beyond the reach of memory
or hope that malign moment un-redeemed
     your light-etched shadow fleeing its
melanoma staining the city's ruined skin
     That didn't stop you arrest halt or faze you
it never gave you much in the way of pause
     for thought now did it? War is peace death
deterrence waste disposable Now you have
     your own concrete shrine your Sunday-best
sarcophagus Chernobyl's hat tipped over a
     scorpion You don't need me to tell you how
all this could end in tears Enough now Enough
     Let me soothe you by saying that I'm merely
what the eye lets in shocked off the retina
     for the brain's collation – solid edges liquid
shapes movement colours textures of hair
     or skin or bark a pewter sky a sunset a
glass of Bordeaux the grey-toned rain
     lulled sea steel's chill a human voice or
face you recognise the instant it recognises
     you I'm fact illusion fantasy this moment
and all time melting to anticipation retro
     spection Now The way you are A million
chemical subtleties of thought that flush
     into those gaps blanks interstices I linger
in then reach across to make your life worth
     living to make your living *life* I'm the past
and its future that childhood flux your
     mother's smell of lavender talc and sweat
that lies half-kindled in memory I'm her
     touch the down on her cheeks the blue
sash she wore that row of Welsh poppies
     planted at the garden border I'm her dry
throat swallowing last words playing their
     regrets into your ear I'm light to the touch
a conjuring trick your father's hands
     mending a broken toy halving an apple
rolling a cigarette I'm his scent of beer
     and sunshine his hands pressing dock
leaves to a sting I'm his skied six volleyed

goal his tie-breaker fizzing with aces I'm
the illusion it mattered who won anything
       in the end anyway I'm the afternoon of
that lost day you recall meeting a lover
       when rain drizzled after a missed bus and
fog dripped from bare trees and you held
       each other for the first time tangled hands
noses lips tongues made clumsy words
       and love in empty rooms the bed sheets
cool to memory's touch A vase of lilies
       pale sepulchral their smell of death and
sex lingering on your fingers the way they
       lingered later on the switch to bring on
lights against the night If it's still there
       still happening in your hallowed God
forsaken human head it's happening
       because I'm here to make it so I'm the
impulse of innocence the way children
       stumble towards everything the way
you run to the future for solace shelter
       redemption Let's admit it – I can be a
real gobshite a charlatan an inveterate
       wanker an incorrigible fraud a tight
fucker a fair-weather friend When
       you die I'll leave without regrets won't
stop to pack or take down curtains or be
       bundled with old clothes into a carrier
bag or hauled to that High Street shop
       that smells of age and old folks' piss
and stale concern I'll simply split move
       on find another gig That's me! Can't
sit still only out for myself I'm genesis
       imagination impulse Art I'm the soft
machine the well-tempered klavier
       the novel the sestina the sonnet the
nocturne the painting the human torso
       lost in centuries of river mud I'm the
dance in the dancer's head happening
       only just before she parts her thighs I'm
Mnemosyne and her daughters – Manhattan

Tokyo Athens London Paris Dubai Rome –
your golden miles dazzling exciting
    electrifying I'm the world as it is as it
was as it could be I'm the moment and
    its after-shock If there is a future for you
then it will be mine I'm out there in that
    elasticating universe (or is it shrinking or
merely changing shape?) where God is
    shaking out a duster of stars stirring
that dark matter dark energy invisible
    in all the space of Space I'm the human
mind on the verge of collapse the human
    spirit gaseous with unspeakable joy I'm
catatonia a black dog depression freedom
    and servitude I'm an eye-shining mania
the suicide's coin rattling in the meter
    his light to see the darkness by life's
unpaid bill the surcharge the bright
    Exit sign the torch of death the very
depth of life crackling in the gentian-blue
    air of Earth Come closer You with so
much to learn Me with so much to teach
    Come closer Only connect!

Acknowledgements

Acknowledgements are due to the editors of the following magazines where some of these poems first appeared: *Poetry Review, Envoi, Poetry Wales, The North, The London Magazine, The Long Poem Magazine, The Rialto.*

'The Work of Water' was commissioned by the Cumbria Floods Project and displayed in the town centre along with the work of other poets in 2010.

'Drought' was commissioned by the British Council Switzerland for their anthology *Feeling the Pressure*, 2008.

'Electricity' was originally commissioned as part of the Creative Scientist writing project at Belmont Arts Centre, Shrewsbury in 2001.

Also by Graham Mort

A Country On Fire
A Halifax Cider Jar
Into the Ashes
Sky Burial
Snow from the North
Circular Breathing
A Night on the Lash
Visibility: New and Selected Poems
Touch (short stories)